What Do I Do When ...

I'M UNSURE!

Danielle Haynes

PowerKiDS press

PK Beginners

I'm unsure. I don't know what to do.

I'm still learning how to do things on my own.

What should I wear?
I can't decide.

Mom says it's raining.
I should wear a coat!

Sometimes when I'm unsure, I get scared.

I'm unsure if I can trust a stranger.

My parents said to ask for help when I'm unsure.

The police and my mom are safe.

Teachers can also help.

It's OK to be unsure.
Just ask for help.

It's how I learn to make good choices.

Published in 2026 by The Rosen Publishing Group, Inc.
2544 Clinton Street, Buffalo, NY 14224

First Edition

Editor: Danielle Haynes
Book Design: Jeffrey Taylor

Photo Credits: Cover Wpadington/Shutterstock.com; p. 3 Jihan Nafiaa Zahri/Shutterstock.com; p. 5 wavebreakmedia/Shutterstock.com; p. 7 Irina WS/ Shutterstock.com; p. 9 Volurol/Shutterstock.com; p. 11 Inna_Kandybka/Shutterstock.com; p. 13 Natalia Deksbakh/Shutterstock.com; p. 15 fizkes/Shutterstock.com; p. 17 O.PASH/Shutterstock.com; p. 19 Rido/Shutterstock.com; pp. 21, 23 Iryna Dincer/Shutterstock.com.

Cataloging-in-Publication Data
Names: Haynes, Danielle.
Title: I'm unsure! / Danielle Haynes.
Description: Buffalo, New York : PowerKids Press, 2026. | Series: What do I do when…
Identifiers: ISBN 9781499456011 (pbk.) | ISBN 9781499456028 (library bound) | ISBN 9781499456035 (ebook)
Subjects: LCSH: Uncertainty--Juvenile literature. | Decision making--Juvenile literature. | Emotions in children--Juvenile literature.
Classification: LCC BF463.U5 H39 2026 | DDC 155.4124--dc23

Manufactured in China

CPSIA Compliance Information: Batch #QWPK26. For further information contact Rosen Publishing at 1-800-237-9932.